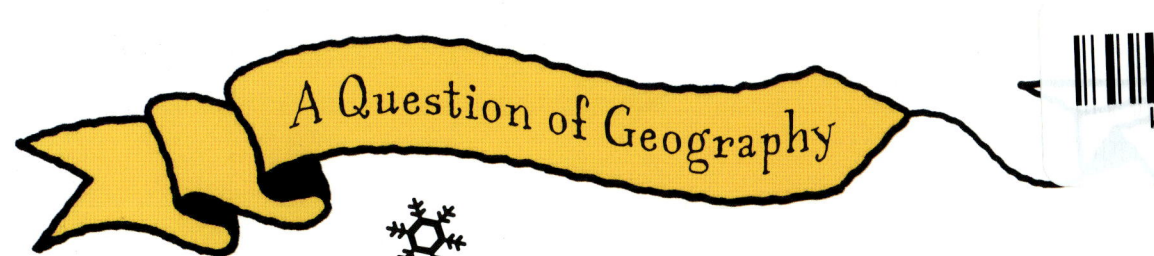

A Question of Geography

Why don't bees freeze in the Arctic?

and other
questions about
BIOMES

Clive Gifford

WAYLAND

First published in Great Britain in 2025
by Wayland

© Hodder and Stoughton, 2025

Credits:
Editors: Julia Bird; Julia Adams
Design and illustrations: Matt Lilly
Cover design: Matt Lilly

HB ISBN 978 1 5263 2533 4
PB ISBN 978 1 5263 2539 6

Printed and bound in Dubai

MIX
Paper | Supporting
responsible forestry
FSC® C104740
FSC
www.fsc.org

Picture credits:

Alamy: Martin Harvey 7t; Adisha Pramod 12b.
Nature PL: Paul Williams 19b.
Shutterstock: John A Anderson 24cr; Steve Bower 11b;
Brandon B 28t; Tony Brindley 21t; Rich Carey 24t;
Dominic Gentilcore PhD 23c; Greens and Blues 24cl;
imageBROKER.com 11t; Javarman 5t; Katvic f cover, 1,14c;
Breck P Kent 9; Leungchopan 15t; Muratart 22-23b;
Nice Kim 20b;Nikolay007 26b; Belikova Oksana 16b;
Paulina Wietrzy-Pelka 29b;Elena Pochesneva 17br; Rehdan 26c;
Alexandre Rosa 7b; Jaume Roselloc 8; Elisei Shafer 25;
Smelov 6t; Ali A Suliman 22c; Usanee 18b; Vladsilver 5b;
Vlad61 24c; Oleg Znamenskiy 6b.

Every attempt has been made to clear copyright.
Should there be any omission please apply
to the publisher for rectification.

Wayland
An imprint of
Hachette Children's Group
Part of Hodder and Stoughton
Carmelite House
50 Victoria Embankment
London EC4Y 0DZ

An Hachette UK Company
www.hachette.co.uk
www.hachettechildrens.co.uk

The authorised representative in the EEA is Hachette Ireland,
8 Castlecourt Centre, Dublin 15, D15 XTP3,
Ireland (email: info@hbgi.ie)

Contents

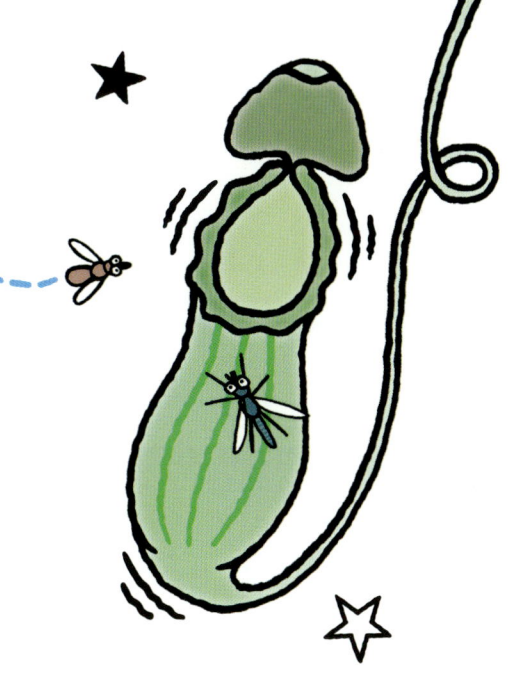

4-5
What on Earth is a biome?

6-7
Which is the grandaddy of all deserts?

8-9
Why don't bees freeze in the Arctic?

10-11
Which rainforest plants are a bit ... clingy?

12-13
Do yeti crabs live up mountains?

14-15
How does a leaf know it's autumn?

16-17
Why is a giraffe's neck soooo long?

18-19
Are there plants that really eat poo?

20-21
Which bird enjoys two summers a year?

22-23
Which animal doesn't drink for ten years?

24-25
Which animal is rock-hard?

26-27
Who clears up a forest's rubbish?

28-29
Quick-fire questions

30-31
Glossary / Further reading

32
Index

What on Earth is a biome?

Our planet is incredibly diverse. Different creatures live together in regions that each have their own landscape, plants and climate. These regions are known as biomes.

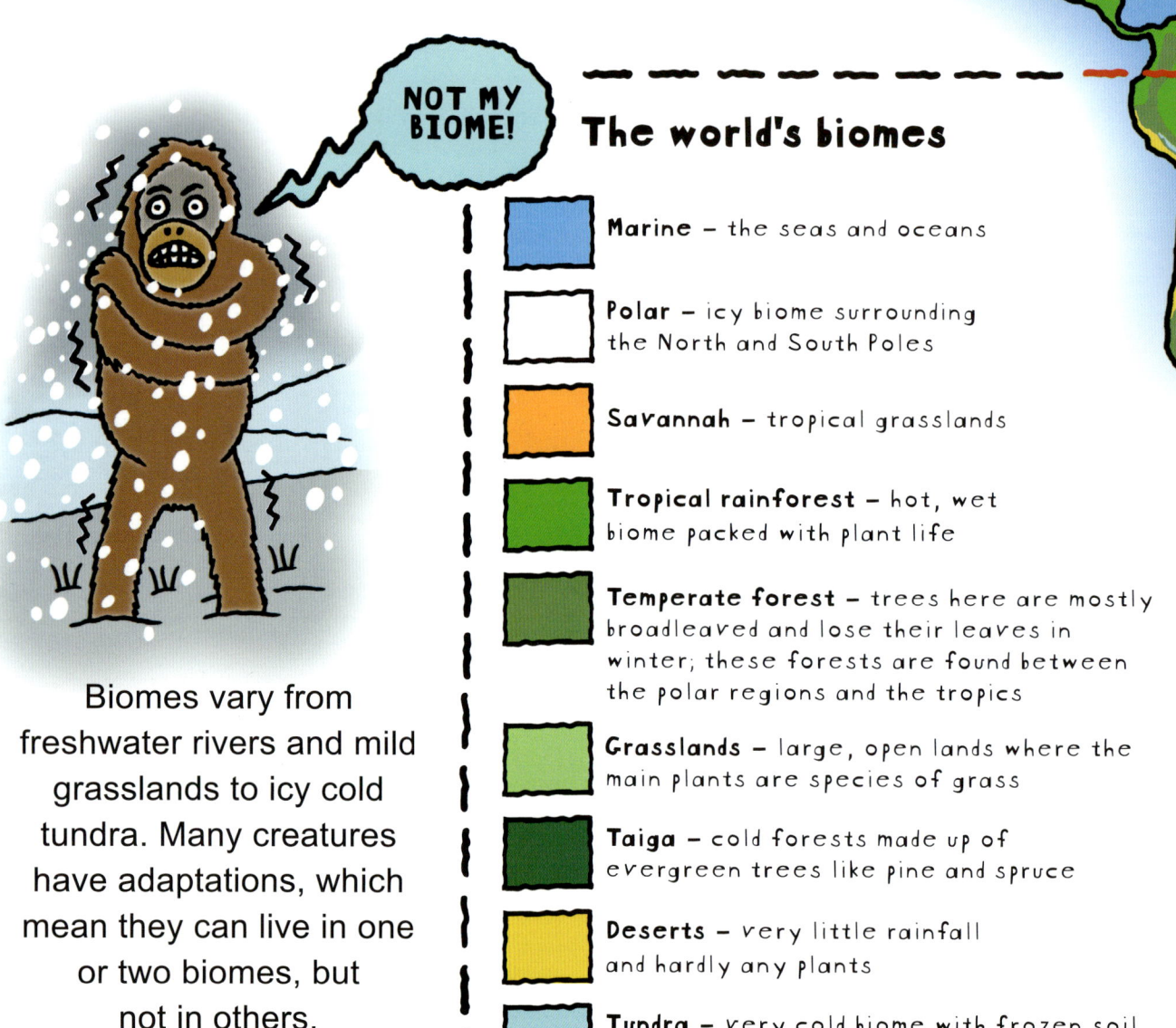

NOT MY BIOME!

Biomes vary from freshwater rivers and mild grasslands to icy cold tundra. Many creatures have adaptations, which mean they can live in one or two biomes, but not in others.

The world's biomes

Marine – the seas and oceans

Polar – icy biome surrounding the North and South Poles

Savannah – tropical grasslands

Tropical rainforest – hot, wet biome packed with plant life

Temperate forest – trees here are mostly broadleaved and lose their leaves in winter; these forests are found between the polar regions and the tropics

Grasslands – large, open lands where the main plants are species of grass

Taiga – cold forests made up of evergreen trees like pine and spruce

Deserts – very little rainfall and hardly any plants

Tundra – very cold biome with frozen soil, low rainfall and short plants

The climate and plants of the savannah biome support large herds of grazing animals and the big cats that prey on them.

Equator

Deserts usually receive less than 250 mm of rain or snow a year. They can be hot, like the Sahara, or cold, like Antarctica.

WHAT'S THE BIGGEST BIOME?

WISH IT WOULD SNOW ...

Easy. It's the marine biome that includes all the world's seas and oceans. The oceans cover 70 per cent of the planet and can plunge to depths of over 10,000 m.

Biomes are amazing and so varied! The best way to find out about biomes is to ask questions, so let's start asking.

Which is the grandaddy of all deserts?

That title goes to Africa's **Namib Desert**, which started forming 56 million years ago. That's almost a million times older than Earth's youngest desert, the Aralkum, which is only 60 years old!

Keeping it cool

Coastal deserts form where there is a cold ocean current close to shore. This cools the air above, stopping it from holding enough water to form clouds that travel over the land and release rain.

ARE WE THERE YET?

The Namib is an ancient coastal desert spanning an area of 80,000 km – more than twice the size of Switzerland. Some parts receive less than 1 cm of rain a year. Sand in this ancient desert has been blown into some truly **GIGANTIC** dunes.

Namib's 170-m-tall Dune 45 is formed of sand that is 5 million years old.

Foggy fact

The Namib receives very little rain, but lots of morning fog, and the fog beetle takes advantage. It performs a handstand to let the tiny water droplets in the fog condense on its body, then trickle down towards its mouth.

AH, THAT'S REFRESHING.

New desert alert!

Since the 1960s, water has been diverted away from the Aral Sea, a large inland sea in Uzbekistan and Kazakhstan, to water crops.

The Aral Sea has now shrunk to one-tenth of its former size. And with little rain falling in the area, the dried-up sea bed has turned into a 45,000-km^2 desert, bigger than Denmark. Covered in low sand dunes and salt flats, the Aralkum is the only large desert created by humans.

Kazakhstan

border

Uzbekistan

Aral Sea today

Aralkum
(Aral Sea before the 1960s)

LOOKS LIKE WE'RE GOING TO HAVE TO WALK!

The Aral Sea used to modify the local climate. With most of its water gone, winters in the desert have become colder, and summers hotter.

Why don't bees freeze in the Arctic?

The tundra and taiga biomes, found inside the Arctic Circle, can be bitterly cold. How does the tiny Arctic bumblebee survive there?

During the short plant-growing season in the Arctic summer, these bees try to stay in the Sun as they **BUZZ** from flower to flower. They gather as much pollen and nectar as possible for their colony before winter returns.

Here are the adaptations that help keep the Arctic bumblebee warm.

Large flight muscles can be twitched to shiver, generating heat and raising its body temperature up to 38°C – much, much warmer than its surroundings.

BZZZ!

Thick coating of fur around its thorax and abdomen keeps cold out and heat in. **Furry nice!**

Abdomen

Thorax

Bigger than most bees, its chunky body means it can hold in body heat for longer.

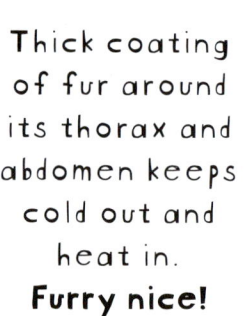

Arctic bumblebees' lives are short. They are born in summer and die in autumn the same year. Only the queen bee survives. She hibernates underground through the winter and restarts the colony by laying eggs the following spring.

BZZZ!

How do other Arctic creatures cope?

As winter approaches, birds and many larger animals leave the Arctic, migrating south to lands with milder winters. Wood frogs cannot travel that far, so they tackle the bitter cold in a different way – they almost stop living!

Most of the frog freezes solid through the winter months. Beforehand, it has pumped glucose sugar throughout its body, which stops ice crystals from growing and damaging its insides.

IT'S NEARLY FREEZE TIME!

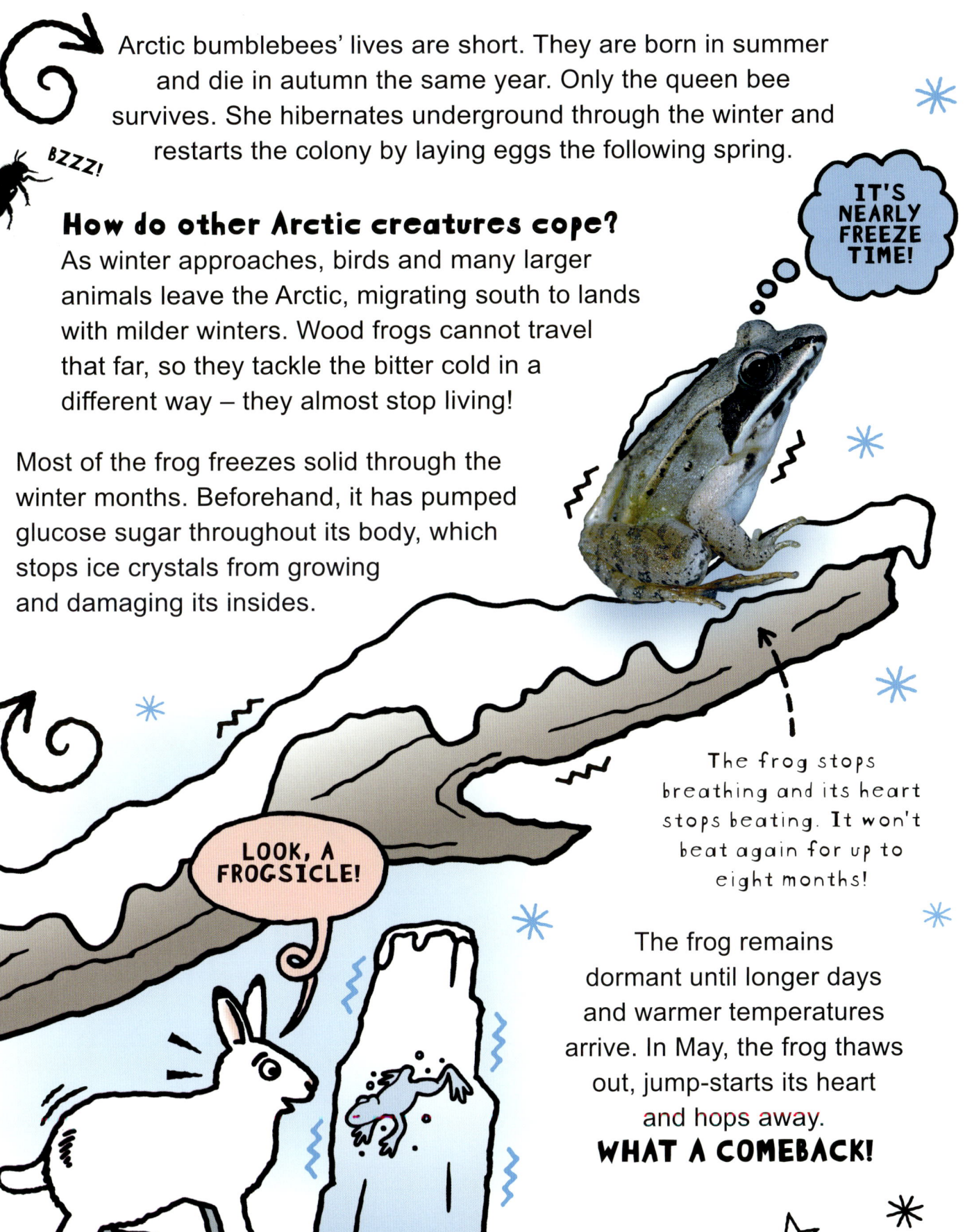

The frog stops breathing and its heart stops beating. It won't beat again for up to eight months!

LOOK, A FROGSICLE!

The frog remains dormant until longer days and warmer temperatures arrive. In May, the frog thaws out, jump-starts its heart and hops away.
WHAT A COMEBACK!

Which rainforest plants are a bit ... clingy?

Warm and wet all year round, tropical rainforests are the perfect biome for plants to grow.

Well, they would be, if it wasn't for all the other plants!

With average temperatures between 20 and 29°C, and more than 200 cm of rain a year, plants grow rapidly. Competition is fierce for nutrients, water and sunlight. Different plants have adopted different solutions to the problem.

OH, THE CANOPY'S THE PLACE TO BE!

The rainforests of South and Central America are home to over 100,000 different species of plant.

WE LIKE IT DARK AND SHADY!

Rainforest rivals

Emergent layer
Emergent trees can grow 60–80 m tall, rising above the canopy to get plenty of sunlight.

Canopy
The canopy is packed with trees and other plants seeking maximum rain and sunlight. It's buzzing with animal life, too.

Understorey
Some understorey plants have giant leaves to catch as much as possible of the sunlight that penetrates the canopy.

Forest floor
Few plants grow on the dark forest floor. Rotting plants and leaves provide food for fungi, worms and insects.

A clingy climb
Many plants want to be in the sunny canopy, but can't develop trunks or stems stiff enough to rise that high. Lianas can reach the canopy by winding around trees for support.

Floating roots
Epiphytes such as orchids grow high above the forest floor on trees. Their roots pick up water vapour and nutrients from the humid air.

Plant pool
Some bromeliads collect water in their bases, providing a mini swimming pool for frogs, insects and even tiny tree snakes.

TIME FOR A SSSSSWIM!

Do yeti crabs live up mountains?

Er, no. Quite the opposite. They are found thousands of metres below sea level in the ocean depths! They are part of a community of odd creatures who rely on deep-sea vents for survival.

Under pressure

Deep ocean waters (anything below 200 m) are tough places to live. Pressure from the water above is intense, there's no sunlight, it's pretty cold and there's little food. Doesn't sound like much fun, does it?

Holiday hotspot

Fortunately, in some places, the ocean floor has openings called hydrothermal vents. These are like hot springs, releasing very hot water, which is rich in minerals.

FURRY NICE TO MEET YOU.

The yeti crab was first discovered in 2006, living 2,200 m below sea level.

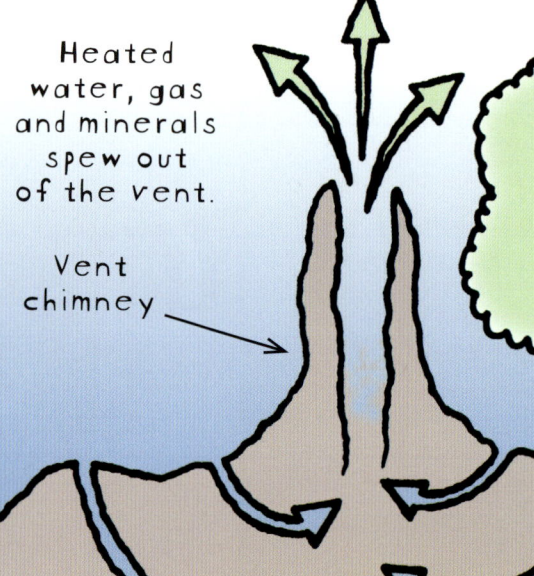

Heated water, gas and minerals spew out of the vent.

Vent chimney

Hydrogen sulphide gas from the vent smells like rotten eggs. **Eww!**

Sea water travels through hot rock.

Heat from magma

Toxic treats

The superhot water exiting a vent is full of toxic chemicals and metals. Some animals around the vents, including giant tube worms and scaly-foot snails, have adapted to use bacteria inside them to convert the chemicals into energy.

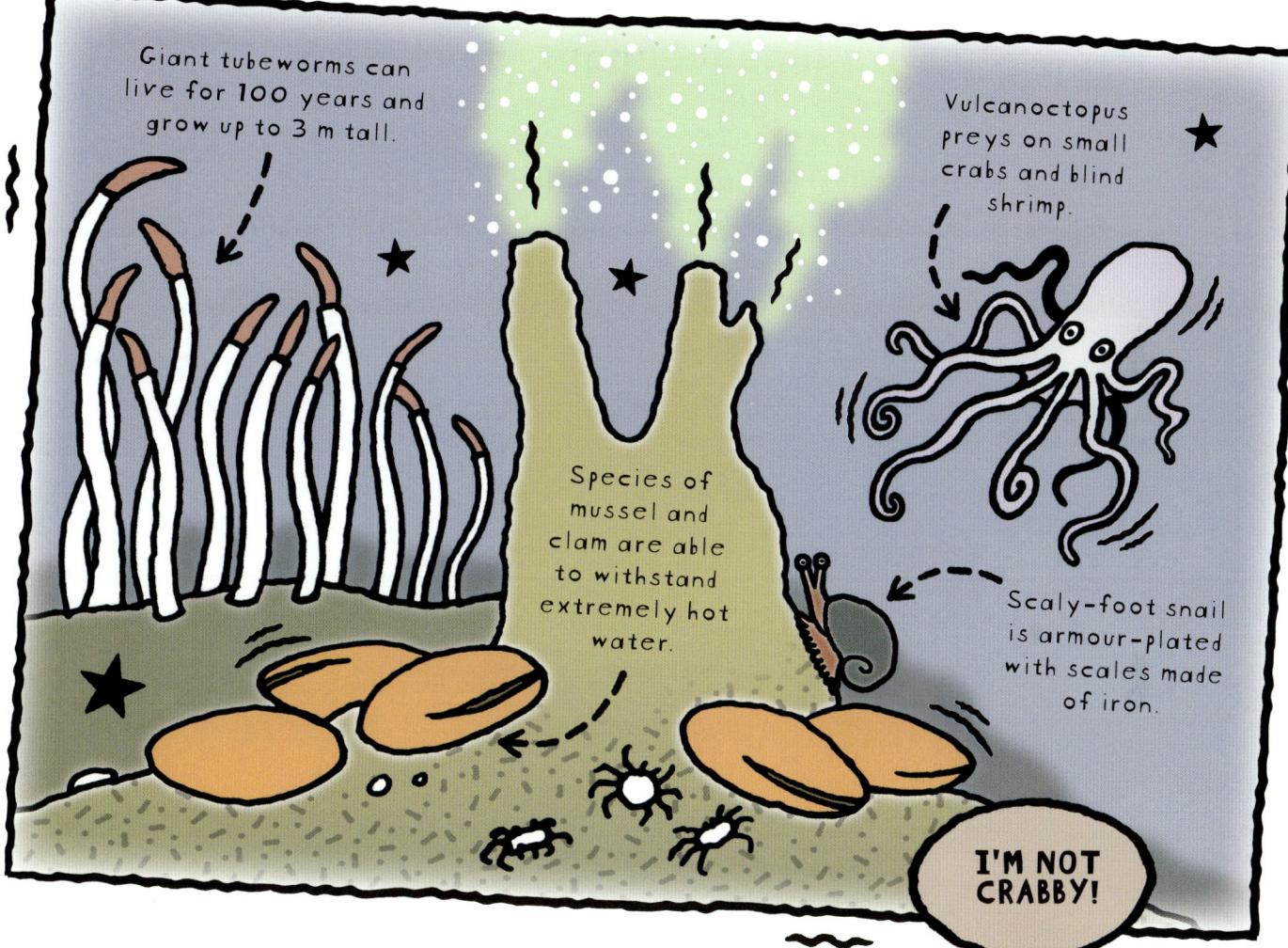

Giant tubeworms can live for 100 years and grow up to 3 m tall.

Vulcanoctopus preys on small crabs and blind shrimp.

Species of mussel and clam are able to withstand extremely hot water.

Scaly-foot snail is armour-plated with scales made of iron.

I'M NOT CRABBY!

So why are they called yeti crabs, then?

Ah, yes. These deep-sea crabs are named after the yeti (the abominable snowman) because they are white and shaggy! They live around hydrothermal vents, gathering bacteria from the water in their hair-like bristles for a tasty snack.

13

How does a leaf know it's autumn?

ALRIGHT, ALRIGHT, I'M GOING!

Each autumn, deciduous trees, such as beech and aspen, lose all their leaves. How do the leaves know when it's time to, ahem, leave?

Temperate forests and woodlands are found north and south of the tropical biomes around the Equator. Here, temperatures are cooler than in the tropics and more variable, with four distinct seasons.

Winter

Spring

Summer

Autumn

A large, mature oak tree may have 600,000 or more leaves.

Food factories

Leaves begin budding and growing in spring. They produce lots of food for the tree via photosynthesis. This takes place thanks to chlorophyll, a substance that gives leaves their green colour.

THIS SEASON'S MUST-HAVE COLOUR IS GREEN ... AGAIN!

Changing colours

When autumn arrives, the tree detects the shorter days, and stops producing chlorophyll. This gives other substances in the leaf (such as orange and yellow carotenes) a chance to be seen. The tree also grows a layer of cells that stops water and nutrients entering the leaves.

BYE, BYE!

OK, I GET THE HINT!

Time to go

The tree gives the leaf a further nudge by no longer making a chemical called auxin. No auxin means cells between the leaf stem and tree weaken, causing the leaf to break off and fall.

Why bother?

Leaves require a lot of effort to keep in tip-top condition. Losing them over the winter allows the tree to conserve energy, water and nutrients, ready for growing new leaves in the spring.

Strong winter winds blow more easily through bare branches. This makes it less likely for the tree to be damaged or uprooted.

I'VE BEEN BLOWN OVER.

Why is a giraffe's neck sooo long?

Savannahs are tropical grasslands found in Africa, Asia, Australia and Central and South America. They provide habitats for lots of life, some of which grows to GIANT sizes.

Africa

Sahara Desert

Savannah

Life on the plain

Africa's savannah consists of giant, rolling plains carpeted with grasses and dotted with small forests or clumps of trees. This land supports herds of grazing animals, such as zebras, antelope and, of course, giraffes.

MUM, WHAT'S FOR PUDDING?

YOUR FAVOURITE ... GRASS!

Zebras eat grass for up to 18 hours a day.

Grasses don't have that much nutritional value, so the big beasts who live there have to chomp their way through a lot of it each day.

Tall story

Giraffes are the tallest animals on Earth, reaching 5.5 m from hoof to head – as tall as three adult men! About 2 m of their height is neck.

Their neck allows giraffes to scan the landscape and gain early warning of predators approaching.

LION ALERT!

DRAT!

I'M NOT GOING UP THERE!

Looking up

Giraffes don't compete with other grass grazers. Instead, they use their great height to gobble up leaves, fruits and shoots on tall acacia, mimosa and wild apricot trees – a food source that other animals, besides the biggest elephants, cannot reach.

Tongue tool

Giraffes use their long tongue to twist, grip and pull branches. It grows up to 53 cm long and is flexible and muscular. Giraffe's tongues and lips work together to strip thorny branches of all their leaves.

SLURP!

Giraffes can eat 35 kg of plants a day.

Are there plants that really eat poo?

Yes! Conditions within a biome vary. **Some areas offer more resources or better living conditions than others. Some plants live where food or space is scarce and solutions have to be found.**

Crowded biome

Tropical forests can be crowded places for plants to access sunlight for photosynthesis (see pages 10–11). So some plants grow in parts where they have little competition for sunlight, but they also don't have access to many nutrients.

OI! WHO SWITCHED THE LIGHTS OFF?

WHERE'S MY LUNCH?

I'M HUNGRY!

Predator plant

There are some 90 species of pitcher plants, which mostly grow in south-east Asian tropical forests. Their leaves curl into a tube (a pitcher), and they have a cunning way of getting a nutrient boost ... **THEY'RE CARNIVOROUS!** Flies and other insects are on the menu.

How they hunt

The pitcher plant attracts its insect prey with bright colours, sweet scents and tasty nectar, found on the pitcher's rim.

JUST A LITTLE CLOSER ...

SLAM!

LET ME OUT!

The insect reaches for the nectar, but the rim is slippery and it falls into the pitcher. The pitcher lid snaps shut. Once in, there's no way out. **GULP!**

BURP!

The base of the pitcher holds digestive juices. These break down the insect's body, so the plant can slowly absorb its nutrients.

Rat catchers

Some pitcher plant species are very big, with pitchers big enough to trap and eat frogs and rats!

And the poo?

Some pitchers also attract rainforest animals that they DON'T eat. The rim of the plant provides a place for tree shrews to perch as they sip the nectar, then go to the toilet inside the pitcher. Urgh!

The plant welcomes the shrew poo, though, as it is packed with nitrogen and other important nutrients. **YUM!**

GOT ANY LOO ROLL?

Which bird enjoys two summers a year?

The tundra is a treeless, icy biome that's not easy to live in. This is especially the case in winter, with temperatures below -20°C, little or no daylight and frozen soil. BRRR.

All change

As its brief, 2–3 month-long summer arrives, the tundra leaps into life. Temperatures head above zero and the days get longer and **L O N G E R** until peak summer, when there's no night time at all. Plants grow rapidly and ice melts, forming shallow lakes and marshes. These wetlands briefly teem with life and provide food for birds … among them, the Arctic tern.

I JUST LOVE CLOCKING UP THE AIR MILES.

I'M A FREQUENT FLYER.

Travelling tern

Terns start the summer in the Arctic biome, where they breed and raise their chicks. After summer ends there, they fly to the other end of Earth, the Antarctic polar biome, to experience a similar summer there. Cheeky!

Fishy flight

The birds follow complex flightpaths, often passing coasts where they can enjoy rich pickings by gliding just above the sea and catching small fish.

Second summer

Once in Antarctica, the birds feast on fish, shrimp and krill found in the icy waters around the coast. After the Antarctic summer's over, they're off again, migrating northwards back to the Arctic summer.

Tireless travellers

Although their routes vary, many Arctic terns fly around 71,000 km a year. No other creature travels as far or experiences as much daylight each year. In fact, during its typical 30-year life, an Arctic tern may fly over 2.1 million km – that's 5.5 times the distance between Earth and the Moon!

Arctic

Antarctic

Which animal doesn't drink for ten years?

Hot, dry deserts can see no rain for months. Some creatures have adapted to living without water for long periods of time.

Camels, for instance, store fat in the hump on their back. They can break down some of this fat into energy and water when it's most needed.

I'VE GOT THE HUMP!

On average, the entire Sahara receives less than 75 mm of rainfall a year.

Desert tortoises carry their own water supply with them, stored in their bladder as wee! Wee is 95–99 per cent water, and the tortoises absorb this water back into their bloodstream when needed.

WE(E) DON'T NEED TO FIND A WATER HOLE.

Rat-tastic!

The kangaroo rat is found in North American deserts and needs incredibly little water to survive. It's packed with features and behaviours that help it survive in a bone-dry desert.

The rat doesn't sweat or pant, even when it's very hot. This means it doesn't lose moisture to the outside air.

Long whiskers are kept in contact with the ground in the dark. This helps the rat feel its way around at night, when it is cooler.

Powerful leg muscles propel the rat to distances of up to 2.75 m to escape snakes – their number one threat.

Short front legs, armed with sharp claws, are used to dig burrows to stay out of the hot sunlight during the day.

Seed solution

Kangaroo rats eat small, dry plant seeds, and lots of them. They keep stores of spare seeds, called caches, in their burrows for when food is scarce.

These seeds are rich in carbohydrates. When the rat's body breaks down carbohydrates to create energy, it also produces water. As a result, many kangaroo rats **NEVER** take a drink throughout their whole, ten-year-long, life. Incredible!

PSSSST, GOT ANY SEEDS?

Kangaroo rats don't even use water for cleaning. Instead, they take a dust bath.

Which animal is rock-hard?

They may feel as solid as rock and grow in branches like plants, but coral are neither! They're actually animals that build their own biome.

I'M HARD AS A ROCK!

Elkhorn

WE ARE, TOO!

Brain coral

HI BUDDING BUDDY!

Lettuce leaf

There are more than 2,000 known species of coral. Some are soft, but many are hard and rock-like.

Budding and building

An individual coral polyp is just 1–10 mm long. It attaches itself to a rock on the sea floor. Polyps divide themselves to form new polyps – a process called budding. This occurs many times throughout their lifetime.

Eating in

Most coral polyps rely on algae living inside them, called zooxanthellae. The algae find a safe home inside the coral and, in return, pass on nutrients to the coral. For coral and zooxanthellae it's a win-win!

ZAP!

OUCH!

Some coral polyps capture plankton and tiny particles of food using microscopic tentacles. They often have stinging cells to stun their tiny prey.

Rock star

As a hard coral grows, it produces a substance called calcium carbonate. This is found inside limestone and other rocks and forms a hard, brittle skeleton on the outside of the coral.

Build-a-biome

A single piece of coral may be made of tens of thousands of polyps, and an entire coral reef may take thousands of years to form. These underwater biomes are packed with life. Although coral reefs cover just 0.1 per cent of the ocean floor, they're home to 25 per cent of all marine species!

Climate change and coral

The Great Barrier Reef near Australia is teeming with around 450 species of hard coral and 1,625 species of fish. But it is under threat. Climate change is causing the reef's waters to warm up, stressing the coral (see page 28).

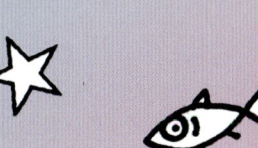

Who clears up a forest's rubbish?

In deciduous forests, millions of leaves fall each autumn. All of this plant matter would pile up and up without nature's own recycling heroes – the decomposers.

Fly agaric toadstool

Breaking down

Decomposers help to break down dead plant matter, turning it into nutrients that enrich the soil. These recyclers include bacteria, earthworms, termites, millipedes and, especially in forests, fungi.

Honey fungus

WE'RE EARTH'S CLEAN-UP CREW!

Fungi are mushrooms and much more! There are over a million different species of these toadstools, moulds and yeasts. Many release chemicals that break down dead plants and wood into nutrients that plants use for growth and repair.

Below the surface

Most of a forest's fungus lies below ground. Its thin threads, called hyphae, grow through soil and wrap around tree roots. Many fungi form partnerships with trees. The tree roots supply fungi with sugars and, in return, the fungi give trees useful nutrients.

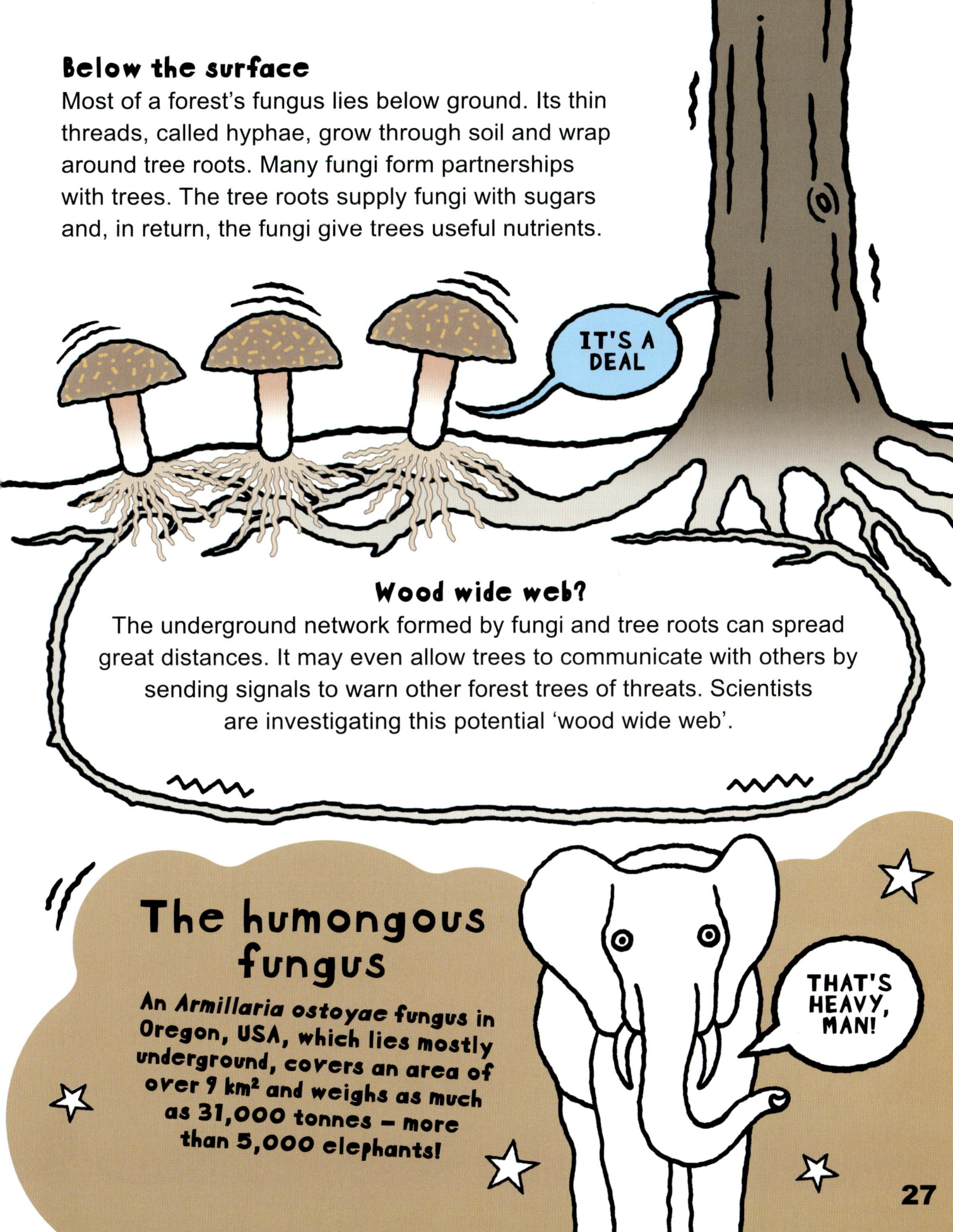

IT'S A DEAL

Wood wide web?

The underground network formed by fungi and tree roots can spread great distances. It may even allow trees to communicate with others by sending signals to warn other forest trees of threats. Scientists are investigating this potential 'wood wide web'.

The humongous fungus

An *Armillaria ostoyae* fungus in Oregon, USA, which lies mostly underground, covers an area of over 9 km² and weighs as much as 31,000 tonnes – more than 5,000 elephants!

THAT'S HEAVY, MAN!

Quick-fire questions

Which desert holds more than half of Earth's freshwater?

Antarctica! This continent is a polar desert, with 99.5 per cent of its surface covered in snow and ice. In fact, it stores over half of all of Earth's freshwater as ice. If all that ice melted, the world's sea levels would rise by 70 m!

Antarctica is a largely lifeless biome that only receives about 150 mm of water in the form of snow every year.

Do corals get stressed?

Yes, warmer waters and pollution can seriously stress coral. This can lead to the algae it relies on to produce its food (see page 24), leaving. As a result, the coral turns white. This bleached coral is vulnerable and may die off through disease or starvation. Thousands of square metres of coral suffer bleaching every year.

Healthy coral

Stressed coral

Where can you find the world's shortest tree?

In the Arctic tundra. The dwarf willow tree never grows taller than the height of your hand (10 cm). Most grow just 1–6 cm high – that's titchy! These ground-hugging mini trees are so low, that they avoid most of the Arctic tundra's bitter winds, while their broad leaves catch as much sunlight as they can.

Which is the most unexplored biome?

Without question, the ocean. It covers 70 per cent of the planet and has an average depth of 3,682 m. That's a **V A S T** area to explore! But people can only explore the top few metres without specialist diving gear or a submersible vehicle that can travel deep underwater.

Marine scientists believe that 90 per cent of all life in the ocean is found in the top 200 m. Yet, there is still plenty of life thriving in the deep, least-explored parts of the ocean.

THERE'S NO LIFE DOWN HERE ...

Glossary

Adaptation A change in a living thing's structure or parts, or a change in their behaviour, that improves the chances of survival. The adaptations that work best are passed on to new generations.

Bacteria Microscopic, single-celled living things.

Biome A community of plants and animals living together in a particular climate and landscape.

Carnivorous Describing an animal or plant that gains their food and energy from eating meat.

Chlorophyll A green pigment found in plants, necessary for carrying out photosynthesis.

Climate The average weather conditions of an area over many years, as measured by temperature, wind speed, rain and snowfall.

Climate change Changes in long-term weather patterns and average temperatures.

Condense When a gas or vapour cools and turns into a liquid.

Deciduous Used to describe species of trees that lose their leaves in the autumn.

Decomposer An organism that lives on dead things and helps break them down.

Drought A period of dryness and shortage of water, which, if it continues for a long time, can cause plants and animals to die.

Environment The surroundings in which a person, plant or animal lives, including the air, water and land.

Equator An imaginary circle around Earth that lies halfway between the North and South Poles.

Hibernate When a creature passes winter in a resting state.

Nectar A sugary, sweet liquid produced by flowers to attract creatures that may help with pollination.

Nutrient A substance that plants and animals need to live and grow.

Photosynthesis The process by which plants use light, carbon dioxide and water to make food.

Pollinate When a creature, wind or water transfers pollen grains to a female part of a plant, so that they can produce seeds.

Species A group of living things of the same kind that can potentially breed with one another.

Further reading

Websites

thewildclassroom.com
In-depth information and images of each biome,
from Arctic tundra to hot desert.

blueplanetbiomes.org
Click on the world map and explore each of the world's major biomes.

askabiologist.asu.edu/explore/Virtual-360-Biomes
Enjoy exploring scenes of different biomes in 360° vision
at this Arizona University website.

earthobservatory.nasa.gov/biome
Learn more about each biome and play a fun game
where you get to match the plant to its biome!

youtube.com/watch?v=V5VYYBR6M6Q&t=2s
Take a virtual dive through part of the Great Barrier Reef
off the coast of Australia.

wildearthlab.com/2023/06/28/desert-adaptations/
Learn more about different adaptations creatures have
developed to survive in hot deserts.

Books

Geographics: Biomes
by Izzi Howell (Franklin Watts, 2019)

The Incredible Ecosystems of Planet Earth
by Rachel Ignotofsky (Wren & Rook, 2019)

Big Planet
by Jon Richards (Franklin Watts, 2024)

Index

A
adaptations 4, 8–9, 13, 22
algae 24, 28
Antarctica 5, 20–21, 28
Aral Sea 7
Arctic 8–9, 20–21, 29
Arctic bumblebees 8–9
Arctic terns 20–21

B
bacteria 13, 26
beetles 7

C
camels 22
carnivorous plants 18–19
climate 4–5, 7
climate change 25
coast 6, 21, 28
corals 24–25, 28

D
decomposers 11, 26
deep ocean 12–13, 29
deserts 4–7, 16, 22–23, 28
    Aralkum 6–7
    Namib 6–7
    Sahara 5, 16, 22

F
forests (temperate) 4,
    14–15, 26–27
frogs 9, 11, 19
fungi 11, 26–27

G
giraffes 16–17
grasslands 4, 16–17
Great Barrier Reef 25

H
hydrothermal vents 12–13

K
kangaroo rats 23

L
lianas 11

M
magma 12
marine biome 4, 12–13,
    24–25, 29
migration 9, 20–21

O
oceans 4–6, 12–13, 24–25,
    28–29
orchids 11
overwintering 9

P
pitcher plants 18–19
polar biome 4–5, 28
predators 17–18

R
rainforests (tropical) 4,
    10–11, 18–19

S
savannas 4–5, 16–17
shrews 19
sunlight 10–12, 18, 29

T
taiga 4, 8–9
trees 4, 11, 14–17, 27, 29
    deciduous 14–15, 26–27
    evergreen 4
tundra 4, 8–9, 20–21, 29

W
wood wide web 27

Y
yeti crabs 12–13

Z
zebras 16